Discover
EXODUS
OUT OF OPPRESSION

by
Carol Veldman Rudie

FAITH
ALIVE®
Christian Resources

Grand Rapids, Michigan

We thank Carol Veldman Rudie of Minneapolis, Minnesota, for writing this study.

Cover photo: PhotoDisc, Inc.

We welcome your comments. Call us at 1-800-333-8300 or e-mail us at editors@faithaliveresources.org.

ISBN 1-56212-238-X

10 9 8 7 6 5 4

Contents

How to Study 4

Introduction 5

Glossary of Terms 6

Lesson 1:
The Egyptian Scene 8

Lesson 2:
A Deliverer Is Born 10

Lesson 3:
Moses' Commission 13

Lesson 4:
Hesitant Preparation 16

Lesson 5:
The Opening Round 19

Lesson 6:
The Lord of Israel 22

Lesson 7:
Blood, Frogs, and Gnats 25

Lesson 8:
Four More Plagues 27

Lesson 9:
The Final Blows 30

Lesson 10:
Passover 33

Lesson 11:
Leaving Egypt 36

Lesson 12:
In a Tight Spot 38

Lesson 13:
Victory Achieved 41

Evaluation Questionnaire

How to Study

The questions in this study booklet will help you discover for yourself what the Bible says. This is inductive Bible study—in which you will discover the message for yourself.

Questions are the key to inductive Bible study. Through questions you search for the writers' thoughts and ideas. The questions in this booklet are designed to help you in your quest for answers. You can and should ask your own questions too. The Bible comes alive with meaning for many people as they discover the exciting truths it contains. Our hope and prayer is that this booklet will help the Bible come alive for you.

The questions in this study are designed to be used with the New International Version of the Bible, but other translations can also be used.

Step 1. Read each Bible passage several times. Allow the ideas to sink in. Think about their meaning. Ask questions about the passage.

Step 2. Answer the questions, drawing your answers from the passage. Remember that the purpose of the study is to discover what the Bible says. Write your answers in your own words. If you use Bible study aids such as commentaries or Bible handbooks, do so only after completing your own personal study.

Step 3. Apply the Bible's message to your own life. Ask,
- What is this passage saying to me?
- How does it challenge me? Comfort me? Encourage me?
- Is there a promise I should claim? A warning I should heed?
- For what can I give thanks?

If you sense God speaking to you in some way, respond to God in a personal prayer.

Step 4. Share your thoughts with someone else if possible. This will be easiest if you are part of a Bible study group that meets regularly to share discoveries and discuss questions. If you would like to learn of a study group in your area or if you would like more information on how to start a small group Bible study,
- write to Discover Your Bible at

2850 Kalamazoo Ave. SE	or	P.O. Box 5070
Grand Rapids, MI 49560		STN LCD 1
		Burlington, ON L7R 3Y8

- call toll-free 1-888-644-0814, e-mail *smallgroups@crcna.org*, or visit *www.SmallGroupMinistries.org* (for training advice and general information)

- call toll-free 1-800-333-8300 or visit *www.FaithAliveResources.org* (to order materials)

Introduction

The first fifteen chapters of Exodus comprise one of the most important stories of the Bible. These chapters reveal the character of God and his attributes. They also picture God as the divine redeemer and the people of Israel as the nation through whom he would bring his saving love to the entire world. In short, these chapters detail God's plan to save.

The Exodus narrative is a continuation of Genesis. As the story opens, Abraham's descendants become enslaved to a ruthless Egyptian pharaoh who despises them. Their situation steadily deteriorates until hope is born in the person of Moses. God chooses and sends Moses (3:10) to be a mediator, to lead the people out of Egypt to freedom.

This story tells us a great deal about Moses and about God. Moses' spiritual biography as well as his political activity demonstrate that faithfully following the Lord brings dramatic results. We also see that the God whom Moses comes to trust is not an ordinary deity. In the Exodus narrative, God demonstrates repeatedly how much he cares for his people. His strength, power, knowledge, and protection prove him to be the God above all gods.

However, Moses faces great opposition at the hands of a mighty pharaoh who refuses to bow to God's authority. Pharaoh denies his slaves freedom to serve their God, for to do so would be to acknowledge the supremacy of the Israelites' God over the Egyptian deities. In response, God issues ten dramatic plagues designed to bring judgment upon the Egyptians and, ultimately, salvation for the Israelites.

As you study these lessons, note the weak and helpless condition of the Israelites. They truly are impotent in the face of their oppressor; they can do nothing to gain their salvation. But God keeps his promise to their forefather, Abraham (Gen. 15:13-21). God provides an "exodus" (from the Greek word meaning "the way out") from their slavery. And by preserving them in the face of incredible opposition, he proves that he is worthy to be their God. In final celebration of freedom, the people pledge their allegiance to this awesome God.

The key question of these chapters is "Whom shall we serve—the gods of Egypt or the God of our father, Abraham?" That is a pivotal question for today. Come back to it again and again as you discuss these lessons and help your group members answer it for themselves.

Taken as a whole, the narrative of Exodus mirrors the redemptive plan of God for his children even today. It gives us a fascinating glimpse of God's purpose throughout history, that is, to provide a divine mediator, Jesus Christ, who frees people from enslavement to sin and leads them into a promised land, a spiritual resting place (Heb. 3:1-6; 4:9).

Glossary of Terms

Abraham—the father of the Jewish people, called by God to leave his homeland and begin a family of people who would be faithful to the Lord and live in the land of Canaan.

Canaanites—the inhabitants of Canaan [present-day Israel], the land that the Lord had promised to give to Abraham and his descendants.

circumcision—the Jewish rite, established by God in covenant with Abraham, of removing the foreskin of the penis from male infants when they were eight days old as the sign of belonging to God's covenant people.

consecrate—to set apart for holy purposes; to dedicate to God.

covenant—a mutually binding agreement imposed by rulers on their subjects, in this case by the Lord upon his people. Both have certain rights and responsibilities. God made the first Jewish covenant with Abraham. In it God promised to give to Abraham's descendants their own land and to be their God. The people were to live lives totally consecrated to God.

exodus—exit, departure, literally "the way out."

Goshen—the land given to Jacob and his family when they came to live in Egypt. It was located on the eastern side of the Nile delta in northern Egypt. Later, Jacob's descendants inhabited Goshen while they were enslaved by the Egyptians.

Hebrew—a general term for the descendants of Abraham; commonly used by foreign nations when referring to the Israelites.

hyssop—a bush with many small, closely packed branches useful for sweeping.

Isaac—the son of Abraham from whom the Jewish people descended.

Israel—another name for Jacob (Ex. 1). Later it is used exclusively to designate all the people who descended from Jacob's twelve sons; the nation of Israel.

Jacob—Isaac's son who received the Lord's original promise to Abraham. The descendants of Jacob's twelve sons became the twelve tribes of the people of Israel. Jacob was renamed Israel by the Lord.

Joseph—one of the twelve sons of Jacob who, after being sold into Egyptian slavery by his brothers, became a prominent official in Pharaoh's court. During a severe famine he saved his entire family by moving them to Egypt where there was food. When Joseph died, he asked that his bones be taken back to Canaan when the Israelites returned there.

mediator—one who seeks to achieve reconciliation between two parties.

Midian—desert region, east of Egypt, inhabited by nomadic shepherds. The precise location is uncertain.

Moses—the man chosen by God to lead his people out of Egypt to the borders of the promised land of Canaan. During his leadership he received from God and taught Israel the laws that would govern them as God's chosen people.

Pharaoh—the title used by the kings of Egypt. These kings were believed to be sons of the gods and therefore divine in their own right. Their word was the law of the land.

plunder—to take the goods of another (usually) by force as in war.

redeem—to buy something back; to save something from destruction by offering something valuable in exchange; to deliver someone from evil by the payment of a price, called a ransom. The Israelites were redeemed from certain death in Egypt by the blood of the Passover lamb. It was a price paid by God, not to the Egyptians, but to satisfy his own justice. Redemption from certain spiritual death was bought for all who believe by the blood of Jesus Christ shed on the cross of Calvary.

remember—to express concern or loving care for another.

spelt—a wheat-like grass.

vigil (to keep vigil)—to keep watch or guard when sleep is customary.

Lesson 1
Exodus 1:1-22

The Egyptian Scene

1. *Exodus 1:1-5*

   Israel was a name given by God to Jacob, one of the early ancestors of the Jews. His descendants were called Israelites. When a famine ravaged their world, the entire family traveled from Canaan (present-day Israel) to Egypt, where much food had been stored.

   As the book begins, what do we learn about the sons of Israel?

2. *Exodus 1:6-7*

   What happened to the people while they lived in Egypt?

3. *Exodus 1:8-10*

   What does the new king fear? Why?

4. *Exodus 1:11-14*

   a. What do the Egyptians do as a result of their new king's assessment?

   b. What are the effects on the Israelites?

5. *Exodus 1:15-16*

   What is the king's next order?

6. *Exodus 1:17-19*

   a. How do the midwives respond to the king's order?

   b. Why do they respond this way?

7. *Exodus 1:20-22*

   a. How does God respond to the midwives?

   b. How does God honor their obedience?

   c. What does Pharaoh order his people to do?

Summary

   a. Which two powers are in opposition in Exodus 1?

   b. Has Pharaoh been successful in controlling the Israelites? Why?

Lesson 2
Exodus 2:1-25

A Deliverer Is Born

1. *Exodus 2:1-4*

   a. What decisions does the Levite woman make?

   b. Why does she act as she does?

2. *Exodus 2:5-6*

   a. Describe the discovery of the baby.

   b. What kind of person finds the baby?

3. *Exodus 2:7-10*

   a. What does the baby's sister do to guarantee his survival?

   b. In what ways is the growing child both Hebrew and Egyptian?

4. *Exodus 2:11-14*

   a. How does Moses identify with the Hebrew people?

   b. What do these accounts tell us about Moses?

5. *Exodus 2:15-17*

   a. What does Pharaoh attempt to do? How does Moses respond?

   b. What does Moses do in Midian?

6. *Exodus 2:18-22*

   a. How did Reuel respond when his daughters return?

   b. How does Moses' life change in Midian?

   c. What is the significance of the name of Moses' son?

7. *Exodus 2:23-25*

    a.   What happened in Egypt while Moses lived in Midian?

    b.   What do we learn about God in these verses?

    c.   What does God remember?

Summary

    a.   How do the three environments of Hebrew home, Egyptian palace, and Midianite tent contribute to Moses' development?

    b.   What character traits does Moses have?

    c.   What has God been doing during this time?

Lesson 3

Exodus 3:1-22

Moses' Commission

1. *Exodus 3:1-3*

    a. What is Moses' situation at this time?

    b. How does God appear to Moses?

2. *Exodus 3:4-6*

    a. What does God ask Moses to do?

    b. What does God do as Moses comes closer?

    c. How does Moses respond? Why does he hide his face?

3. *Exodus 3:7-10*

    a. How does the Lord describe the Israelites?

b. What does God command Moses to do for Israel? Why?

4. *Exodus 3:11-12*
   a. How does Moses respond to God's call? Why?

   b. How does God reassure him?

5. *Exodus 3:13-14*
   a. What is Moses' next concern?

   b. How does God identify himself?

   c. How is this identification different from his identification in verse 6?

6. *Exodus 3:15-17*
   a. How is Moses to identify God to the Israelites?

   b. How has the Lord already shown his favor to the Israelites?

7. *Exodus 3:18-20*
    a. How will Moses be received by the elders?

    b. What are they to say to Pharaoh? How will he respond?

    c. What action does the Lord promise?

8. *Exodus 3:21-22*
    How will the Lord enrich the departing Israelites?

Summary
    a. What does Moses learn about God's character and identity?

    b. What will account for the success of the task to which God is calling Moses?

Lesson 4

Exodus 4:1-26

Hesitant Preparation

1. *Exodus 4:1-5*

   a. How does Moses respond to the Lord's previous promises?

   b. What does the Lord give Moses in response?

2. *Exodus 4:6-9*

   a. What is the second sign that the Lord gives Moses?

   b. How does the third sign differ from the first two?

3. *Exodus 4:10-12*

   a. What excuse does Moses offer next?

   b. What is the Lord's response?

4. *Exodus 4:13-17*

    a. What is Moses' final plea?

    b. How does God respond?

    c. How will Aaron assist Moses?

5. *Exodus 4:18-20*

    a. How does Moses indicate that he is following the Lord's command?

    b. How is Moses encouraged in his plans?

    c. What does Moses take with him?

6. *Exodus 4:21-23*

    a. What must Moses do when he arrives in Egypt?

    b. What will result from Moses' and Pharaoh's confrontation?

c.   How much does the Lord value Israel?

7.   *Exodus 4:24-26*
     a.   What does the Lord intend to do to Moses?

     b.   How does Zipporah prevent it?

     c.   What might be the point of this incident?

Summary
     a.   What is the relationship between the Lord's plan and human need?

     b.   What does this chapter teach about God's expectations of his people?

Lesson 5
Exodus 4:27-5:21

The Opening Round

1. *Exodus 4:27-31*

   a. How does Aaron's appearance fulfill the Lord's plan?

   b. How do the Israelites respond to Aaron's message?

2. *Exodus 5:1-5*

   a. What is Moses and Aaron's first demand of Pharaoh?

   b. How does Pharaoh respond?

   c. How does their second request differ from their first?

   d. What is Pharaoh's response to their second request?

3. *Exodus 5:6-9*

    a.   What order does Pharaoh give?

    b.   What assumptions does Pharaoh make about the people?

    c.   What do you think Pharaoh fears?

4. *Exodus 5:10-14*

    a.   What do the slave drivers do in response to Pharaoh's command?

    b.   What does this mean for the people? For the Israelite foremen?

5. *Exodus 5:15-18*

    a.   How do the Israelite foremen appeal for relief?

    b.   What is Pharaoh's response?

6. *Exodus 5:19-21*

    a. How do the Israelite foremen assess their trouble?

    b. Whom do they blame?

Summary

    a. Why do you think Pharaoh did not grant Moses and Aaron's request?

    b. What might be the Lord's purpose in allowing the people to suffer even more?

Lesson 6
Exodus 5:22-7:13

The Lord of Israel

1. *Exodus 5:22-6:1*

    a. What does Moses do next?

    b. What is the Lord's response? What does he promise?

2. *Exodus 6:2-8*

    a. What does the Lord tell Moses about himself?

    b. What is the basis for the Lord's deliverance of Israel?

    c. How will the people know that he is their Lord?

3. *Exodus 6:9-13*

    a. How do the people respond to Moses' report?

b. What does the Lord tell Moses to do next?

c. What is Moses' excuse this time?

d. What is God's final word to Moses and Aaron?

4. *Exodus 6:14-27*
What do you think is the purpose of this genealogy?

5. *Exodus 6:28-7:6*
   a. What roles does God assign to Moses and Aaron?

   b. How are they to carry out those roles?

   c. To what degree do Moses and Aaron obey the Lord?

6. *Exodus 7:8-13*

    a. What is different about the power shown by Aaron and that of the magicians?

    b. Why does Pharaoh not listen?

    c. What lesson is the Lord trying to teach Pharaoh?

Summary

    a. How would you describe the roles of Moses, Pharaoh, and the Lord in the confrontation?

    b. What is God's purpose in the story thus far?

Lesson 7

Exodus 7:14-8:19

Blood, Frogs, and Gnats

1. *Exodus 7:14-19*

   a. How does the Lord describe Pharaoh?

   b. What does the Lord tell Moses to do?

   c. How extensive is the plague?

2. *Exodus 7:20-24*

   What is Pharaoh's response? Why does he respond this way?

3. *Exodus 7:25-8:7*

   a. What demand and warning does the Lord give to Pharaoh?

   b. What is the result of Pharaoh's refusal?

4. *Exodus 8:8-11*

   a. Where does Pharaoh turn for relief from the plague?

   b. What could Pharaoh have learned from this plague?

5. *Exodus 8:12-15*

   How does the Lord answer Moses' prayer?

6. *Exodus 8:16-19*

   a. How do the gnats affect Egypt?

   b. What happens when the magicians try to repeat the plague? What do they realize?

Summary

   a. What patterns do you find in these first three plagues?

   b. How would you describe the Lord as he shows himself in these wonders?

Lesson 8
Exodus 8:20-9:35

Four More Plagues

1. *Exodus 8:20-23*

   a. What does the Lord tell Moses to say to Pharaoh?

   b. How will the Lord deal differently with Goshen?

2. *Exodus 8:24-29*

   a. What is the effect of this plague?

   b. What promise and condition does Pharaoh make to Moses?

   c. How does Moses respond?

3. *Exodus 9:1-7*

   a. How extensive will this plague be?

b. What distinction is made between the Israelite and the Egyptian livestock?

c. How is the Lord described as controlling this plague?

4. *Exodus 9:8-12*
    a. How does this plague come about?

    b. What are the results of this plague?

5. *Exodus 9:13-26*
    a. What is the Lord's purpose in sending the plagues?

    b. What do verses 14-16 show us about God's mercy?

    c. Why did some officials listen to the warning?

    d. What does the full force of this plague do?

6. *Exodus 9:27-35*

    a. What does Pharaoh tell Moses and Aaron? Why does he acknowledge this?

    b. Why does Moses honor Pharaoh's request?

    c. According to Moses, what do Pharaoh and his officials still lack?

    d. What do you learn about Pharaoh, Moses, and the Lord from their actions here?

Summary

    a. What is the Lord teaching Pharaoh and Moses through these plagues?

    b. What have we learned about Pharaoh and Moses in this sequence of plagues?

Lesson 9
Exodus 10:1-11:10

The Final Blows

1. *Exodus 10:1-6*

   a. Why has the Lord hardened Pharaoh's heart?

   b. What plague is promised next? How could Pharaoh avoid this plague?

   c. How extensive will the plague be?

2. *Exodus 10:7-15*

   a. How do the officials react? What does Pharaoh do in response?

   b. For what does Moses ask? What treatment do Moses and Aaron receive as a result of this request?

   c. Why does Pharaoh still refuse to let the people go?

d. By what method does the Lord cause the locusts to come?

3. *Exodus 10:16-23*

   a. How does Pharaoh respond to this plague?

   b. What does the Lord show about himself in his actions?

   c. What is unusual about the plague of darkness?

4. *Exodus 10:24-29*

   a. What restriction does Pharaoh place on the Israelites?

   b. Why does Moses insist that the livestock go too?

   c. How would you describe the conclusion of these negotiations?

5. *Exodus 11:1-8*

   a. Describe the final plague.

b. How will this plague affect the Egyptians? The Israelites?

c. What will the Egyptians learn about the Lord?

6. *Exodus 11:9-10*
   a. Why has Pharaoh disregarded Moses and Aaron's words?

   b. What was the ultimate purpose of hardening Pharaoh's heart?

Summary
   a. What have these final plagues shown Pharaoh about the Lord's rule over the whole earth?

   b. How has Moses' relationship with the Lord grown and developed?

Lesson 10
Exodus 12:1-30

Passover

1. *Exodus 12:1-6*

    a. When and where does the Lord give these instructions to Moses and Aaron?

    b. What kind of animal is to be used? How is it to be treated before slaughter?

2. *Exodus 12:7-13*

    a. What is to be done with the lamb?

    b. What are the people to eat, and how are they to eat it?

    c. How is the lambs' blood used? What will it achieve for the Israelites?

    d. What distinctions does the Lord make between Israel and Egypt? Why does he make these distinctions?

3. *Exodus 12:14-20*

   a. What feast follows Passover? Why are the people to celebrate this feast?

   b. How is the feast to be celebrated?

   c. How important is this feast?

4. *Exodus 12:21-23*

   What guidelines for the Passover does Moses add to the instructions already given by the Lord?

5. *Exodus 12:24-28*

   a. What detail does Moses add to the instructions about when to observe this celebration?

   b. How do the people respond?

6. *Exodus 12:29-30*

    a.   How extensive is this plague?

    b.   How do the Egyptians react to the plague?

Summary

    a.   What is the effect of the final plague on the Egyptians? On the Israelites?

    b.   What place is the Passover feast to have in the lives of the Israelites? Of future generations?

    c.   How would you describe the Lord you have seen at work in these verses?

Lesson 11

Exodus 12:31-13:16

Leaving Egypt

1. *Exodus 12:31-36*

    a. What do Pharaoh and the Egyptian people do after the plague strikes?

    b. How does their response differ from previous reactions?

    c. What do the Israelites receive from the Egyptians before they leave Egypt?

2. *Exodus 12:37-42*

    a. Who and what is included in the journey out of Egypt?

    b. Why are the Israelites to keep a vigil?

3. *Exodus 12:43-51*

    a. What regulations does the Lord add to the Passover? Compare these verses with 12:1-28.

b.   Who may celebrate the Passover? Who is forbidden?

4.   *Exodus 13:3-10*

Note that the first two verses of Exodus 13 will be covered in question 5.

a.   For what feast does Moses repeat instructions?

b.   What functions would this observance have for the Israelites and their children (see verses 8-9)?

5.   *Exodus 13:1-2; 11-16*

a.   What belongs to the Lord (see verse 2)?

b.   What can be redeemed? How are they to be redeemed?

c.   What are the people to tell their children?

Summary

a.   Why might instruction concerning religious observances be such a key part of the exodus?

b.   How has the Lord demonstrated his particular care for his people?

Lesson 12
Exodus 13:17-14:20

In a Tight Spot

1. *Exodus 13:17-22*

    a. How are the people described as they leave Egypt?

    b. What do they take with them from Egypt? Why?

    c. What does the Lord use to guide them?

2. *Exodus 14:1-4*

    a. What does the Lord tell Moses to do?

    b. What does the Lord want Pharaoh to think about the Israelites?

    c. What does the Lord want to accomplish by this ruse?

3. *Exodus 14:5-9*

    a. What changes Pharaoh's mind about having allowed the Israelites to go? What does he do about it?

    b. Describe the Egyptians' military preparations.

4. *Exodus 14:10-12*

    a. How do the Israelites react when they see Pharaoh's army?

    b. What do they prefer at this point? Why?

5. *Exodus 14:13-18*

    a. How does Moses reassure the people?

    b. What must the Israelites do to be saved from the Egyptians? What will the Lord do on their behalf?

    c. What outcome does the Lord promise?

6. *Exodus 14:19-20*

How does the Lord protect his people?

Summary

   a. What movement from fear to faith do you see in this passage? What makes that progression possible?

   b. How might this lesson help you when you find yourself in a tight spot for doing the right thing? What might you expect God to do for you then?

Lesson 13

Exodus 14:21-15:21

Victory Achieved

1. *Exodus 14:21-25*

   a. How does the Lord open a way for the Israelites to escape from the Egyptians?

   b. What do the Egyptians do in response?

   c. What does the Lord do to the Egyptians?

2. *Exodus 14:26-31*

   a. What does the Lord tell Moses to do?

   b. How extensive is the Egyptians' destruction?

   c. What is the response of the Israelites?

3. **Exodus 15:1-5**

   a. Who sings this song and why do they sing it? To whom is it sung?

   b. What words describe the Lord and his actions?

4. **Exodus 15:6-12**

   a. What words describe the Lord in these verses?

   b. What seems to motivate the enemy?

   c. To whom is the Lord compared? How does he compare?

5. **Exodus 15:13-18**

   a. How will the Lord relate to his people?

   b. How will the nations respond when they hear about the Lord? Why?

c.   Where will the Lord bring his people?

6.   *Exodus 15:19-21*
     How does Miriam respond to these events?

Summary

a.   What words describe the Lord as you have seen him in this
     lesson?

b.   Why is the Lord faithful to his people?

c.   How are people to respond to the Lord's salvation?

Evaluation Questionnaire

DISCOVER EXODUS—OUT OF OPPRESSION

As you complete this study, please fill out this questionnaire to help us evaluate the effectiveness of our materials. Please be candid. Thank you.

1. Was this a home group ___ or a church-based ___ program? What church?

2. Was the study used for
   ___ a community evangelism group?
   ___ a community faith-nurture group?
   ___ a church Bible study group?

3. How would you rate the materials?

   Study Guide
   ___ excellent ___ very good ___ good ___ fair ___ poor

   Leader Guide
   ___ excellent ___ very good ___ good ___ fair ___ poor

4. What were the strengths?

5. What were the weaknesses?

6. What would you suggest to improve the material?

7. In general, what was the experience of your group?

Your name (optional) _____

Address _____

8. Other comments:

(Please fold, tape, stamp, and mail. Thank you.)

Faith Alive Christian Resources
2850 Kalamazoo Ave. SE
Grand Rapids, MI 49560